THE ILLUSTRATOR'S LIBRARY

Pen & Ink

THE ILLUSTRATOR'S LIBRARY
Pen & Ink

BY DON BOLOGNESE AND ELAINE RAPHAEL

Franklin Watts
New York   London   Toronto   Sydney
1986

The authors would like to express their gratitude
to Frank Sloan, for his guidance and for his
enthusiastic commitment to their work.

Library of Congress Cataloging in Publication Data

Bolognese, Don.
Pen and ink.

(The Illustrator's library)
Includes index.
Summary: A guide for the novice illustrator to using
pen and ink, including choosing pens, keeping a
sketchbook, trying different techniques, and developing
a personal style.
1. Pen drawing—Technique—Juvenile literature.
[1. Pen drawing—Technique] I. Raphael, Elaine.
II. Title. III. Series.
NC905.B65 1986   741.2'6   86-1552
ISBN 0-531-10133-9

C O N T E N T S

INTRODUCTION   7

CHAPTER 1   9
MATERIALS

CHAPTER 2   19
EXPERIMENTING FOR EFFECTS

CHAPTER 3   29
THE WORLD AROUND US

CHAPTER 4   41
EXPANDING YOUR IMAGINATION

CHAPTER 5   53
SKETCH TO FINISH

INDEX   64

Introduction

Have you noticed that some people tell a story very well? They seem to have a gift for choosing words. They know how to use language to capture and hold the attention of their listeners. Some people can do the same thing with pictures, and this form of storytelling is called illustration.

Storytelling is both ancient and honored. Most of the evidence of the past has come to us through words, songs, and pictures. The artists among the cave dwellers have left us a record of actual hunting scenes. The designers of ancient languages created picture symbols from everyday life. And a thousand years ago, when most people could not read, artists used the glorious colors of stained glass to tell stories from the Bible.

Today these examples of storytelling through pictures are considered great art. But in their own time these pictures were appreciated because they also provided information and entertainment. And today, with our advanced communications, the ability to tell a story well through illustration is more important than ever. The Illustrator's Library is designed to help you be the best storyteller you can be.

Fountain pen (fine point) on visualizing paper

Medium point felt pen and very fine fiber-tipped pen plus broad-tipped gray felt marker

C H A P T E R 1

Materials

No one knows or most likely will ever know when the first pen-and-ink drawing was made. It is safe to say, however, that it was a long time ago. We do know that monks, during the Middle Ages, developed pen and ink for both drawing and lettering. Their pens were goose quills. The tips were shaped into pointed and square nibs and they were used with ink made from common substances to create the detailed drawings and flowing calligraphy that we see in medieval manuscripts. Lampblack, a fine soot that is a by-product of kerosene lamps and candles, was one of the earliest "inks."

Since that time pen and ink has become one of the favorite drawing techniques of all artists. The simple quill pens of medieval times have given way to the hundreds of types of technical, lettering, and drawing pens of today. There are now pens with replaceable points and replaceable ink cartridges. There are even totally disposable pens. Felt pens can make fine lines or they can be used for large, broad strokes—in almost any color of the rainbow.

Inks, too, have increased in variety. Not only are there waterproof and water-soluble inks in a wide range of colors, but there are also specially formulated inks for use in technical pens.

In short, there is hardly a type of drawing that has not had a pen designed especially for it. Whether you are drawing the details of the most delicate flower or trying to capture the running motion of a football player, there is a pen-and-ink combination that will help you do the job.

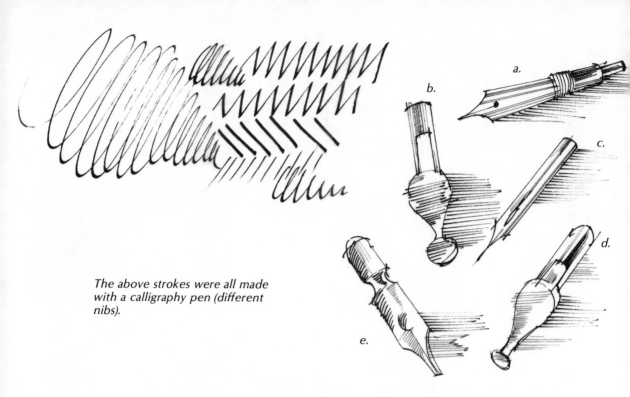

The above strokes were all made with a calligraphy pen (different nibs).

What kind of pen should you use? The best way to decide that is to try several different pen points. Dip pens (pens for dipping into ink) offer the greatest variety of pen points (or nibs) and they are fairly inexpensive. Penholders come in two basic types; the larger of these take most pen points, but for a crow quill or mapping nib you will also need a small penholder.

For sketching away from your desk you will need a fountain pen, a reservoir pen, or a cartridge pen. Most fountain pens use non-waterproof inks and only the more expensive ones have interchangeable points. A reservoir-type pen uses waterproof drawing ink and usually has enough different pen points to provide a variety of line widths.

Cartridge pens, although disposable, are cheaper than reservoir pens. They usually come in superfine, fine, and medium points. They are best for outdoor or location sketching.

Some artists combine the art of lettering with that of illustrations. For this calligraphy, special pens are needed. These calligraphy pens have square nibs that come in graduated widths and the pen can be used both as a dip pen and a fountain pen. One small bit of advice about beginning calligraphy—use non-waterproof ink; it may not be as dark as the waterproof variety but it will give you finer, thin lines.

a.

b.

c.

d.

The points on page 10 are:
a. fountain pen (they come in different sizes
and are interchangeable)
b. round nib (large) dip pen
c. crowquill
d. oval nib (medium) dip pen
e. chisel-edge (calligraphy pen)

Penholders on this page
a. small penholder for crowquill and mapping
pens
b. and c. large penholders
d. fountain pen

The strokes on this page were made with the
points listed above. All drawings were done
on tracing paper.

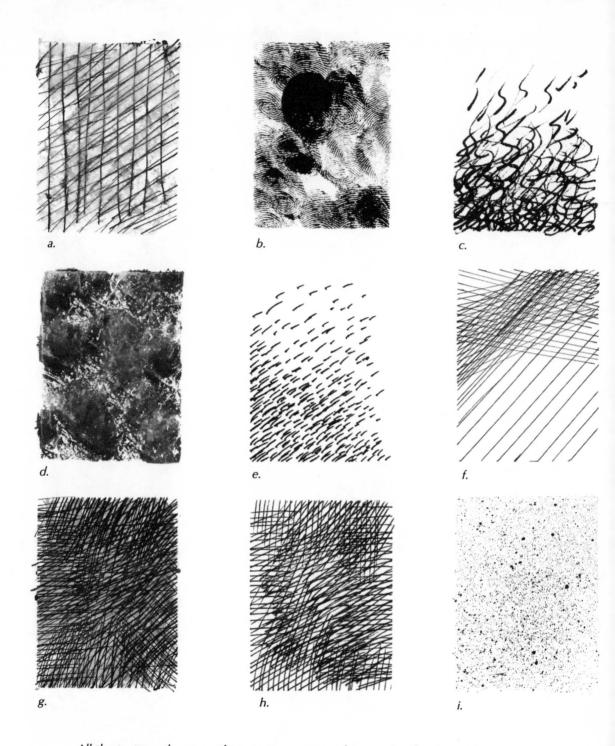

All the textures shown on these two pages were done on Strathmore two-ply kid finish paper: a. fine line with wash; b. fingerprint; c. felt brush pen; d. tissue dipped in ink; e. fountain pen; f. ruling pen; g. fine line; h. fine line wash; i. toothbrush splatter; j. stipple (technical pen); k. ink on cloth pressed on paper; l. brush wash

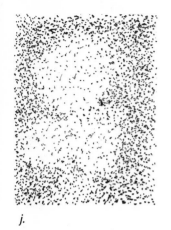

j.

k.

l.

While there are many kinds of pen points, there are really only two basic types of ink, waterproof and non-waterproof (water soluble). Each has advantages and disadvantages. Waterproof ink provides security against accidental smudging due to moisture. It is also easier to correct with white paint since waterproof inks will not bleed through watercolor. On the other hand, waterproof ink cannot be brushed over with water to achieve subtle tones. It also tends to coat pen points more heavily, requiring that you pay more attention to the care of your pens. The chief advantage of non-waterproof inks is that they can be combined with water to produce tones; these inks are especially useful for color.

Paper used for ink drawing needs one important quality; it must have enough sizing (surface coating) to keep the ink from sinking into the fibers. If the paper does not have enough sizing, the ink will blot.

The paper should also have some weight to it; two-ply bristol board, vellum tracing paper, and ledger bond are a few good examples. You can work on thinner paper, but thin paper will buckle from the moisture in the ink. If you've done an ink drawing on paper that buckles, you can save it by mounting the drawing on illustration board. To do that you will need rubber cement and rubber cement thinner.

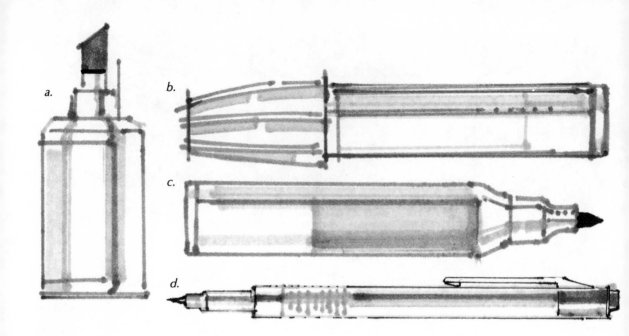

The above drawings were done on non-bleed visualizing paper with the following pens: a. and b. broad-tipped felt marker; c. fine point marker; d. very fine fiber-tipped pen

Felt- and fiber-tipped pens have become very popular with commercial artists. When felt markers were first introduced they were used primarily as design and sketching tools. Eventually better and finer points were developed. That, added to a wide variety of colors, has made the felt pen a much more useful tool.

The felt pen cannot compare to traditional dip pens when it comes to variety; nor can even a superfine felt pen point achieve as thin and clean a line as a very fine technical pen. However, felt pens are relatively inexpensive and very convenient. Illustrators use them primarily for doing a rough sketch or a comprehensive sketch (usually referred to as a "comp"). A "comp" should be a clear representation of what the finished illustration or photograph will look like. For example, the illustration at the top of this page could be a "comp" to show both the photographer and the client (the felt pen manufacturer) how a group of markers will appear in a sales catalog.

Felt pens come in waterproof and water soluble varieties. Both types need to have the caps replaced immediately after use or they will dry up.

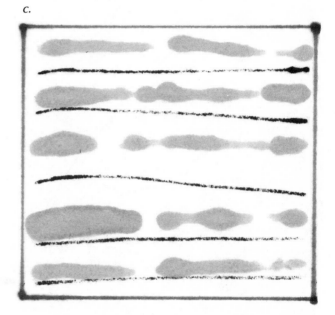

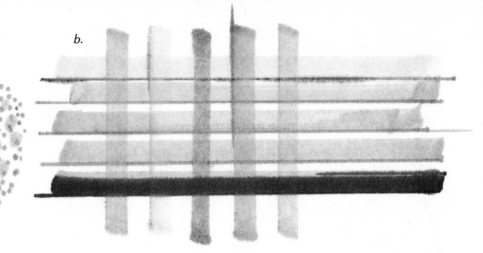

a.

b.

c.

Achieving textures:
a. fine and medium felt-tipped pens (various gray shades) on non-bleed paper
b. felt-tipped pens plus fine felt pen on non-bleed paper
c. fine- and broad-tipped felt pen through tissue paper on to bond paper
d. felt brush marker on bond paper

d.

Drafting tools are designed to do specific jobs associated with engineering and architecture. However, such equipment can also be of great help to the non-technical illustrator. For example, if a very fine line is required, nothing can match a triple O technical pen for precision. And, if you're drawing exact circles, ellipses, or other curved lines, you should use the drafting templates and tools that are available.

Which tools and which templates should you have as a minimum? Certainly, a ruler, several triangles and a T square, one circle and one ellipse template, and a french curve would be a good beginning.

Which pens should you get for technical illustrations? Dip pens are difficult to control against a straight edge or ruler. Ruling pens are excellent with straight edges, difficult with curves, and impossible with templates. Technical pens or very fine fiber pens are the best for templates.

One piece of equipment that is a necessity for the illustrator is the lightbox. Whether you make one yourself (a simple light bulb under a framed piece of frosted glass) or buy one, a lightbox will save you time and help you make the best use of your sketches.

Left and below: *technical pen points with curves, templates, and rulers on ledger bond*

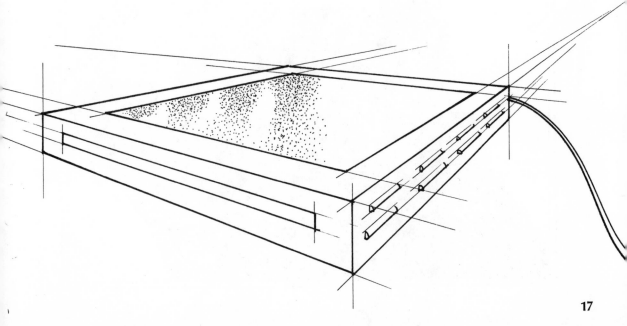

C H A P T E R   2

Experimenting for Effects

Believe it or not, sometimes you can tell what a drawing will look like just by listening! We once worked in a studio with an illustrator who worked with pen and ink. We always knew when she was cross-hatching by the rhythmic scratch-scratch-scratch of her pen; first in one direction, then in another, then another. The longer the scratching continued, the darker the picture would be.

Although it is one of the oldest and most effective pen-and-ink techniques, cross-hatching is only one way of working. There are many other approaches, some that use only line and some that combine wash with pen and ink.

Paper, too, plays an important role in pen-and-ink techniques. The quality of a line is affected by the kind of paper and paper surface on which it is drawn. And line quality—fine, jagged, thick, scratchy, smooth, or splotchy—is essential to the expressiveness of an illustration.

To tell a story through pictures effectively, the illustrator should acquire a good knowledge of the various effects that are possible with a specific medium. The more choices an illustrator has, the greater is his or her ability to choose the right combination of materials for a particular set of illustrations.

Crowquill and technical pen on visualizing paper

Getting started, though, is often difficult. Try the procedure that produced the drawing on page 18. It is a pen-and-ink version of a Renaissance painting. The illustrator's main objective was to see if cross-hatching could be used to render stylized costume design. She also wanted to contrast a simple line with elaborate tones. By working directly from an existing picture, she was able to concentrate on her design experiment. Using previously done work as a starting point for technique and design

a.

b.

experiments is an old and favorite method of learning for students and professionals alike.

You can apply the same method to your own work. These three drawings were all done from the same original. Working on a lightbox, the artist did three versions, each one alike in content and composition but not in technique. The differences demonstrate how important a specific technique is to the overall effect of an illustration.

c.

a. fountain pen (fine point) and technical pen; b. fountain pen and wash; c. fountain pen (fine point) and technical pen. All were done on visualizing paper.

a.

b.

a. Crowquill; b. felt brush pen; c. ball point pen; d. fountain pen (fine point);
e. round point (small) dip pen. a through d were done on visualizing paper;
e was drawn on newsprint

All these cats were drawn by one person, but each was done
with a different pen. Each drawing is so unlike the others that
you might believe that several artists were at work.

Is it possible that simply changing from one pen to another
would make such a difference? Try it. You will see that a pen has
its own character. And you might also discover that you are
more comfortable working with one than with the others. But
before you concentrate on one particular type of pen, try as
many as possible and save the experiments. They will be a good
reminder to you.

c.

d.

e.

23

Waterproof ink on acetate

Ink itself has certain characteristics that lead to interesting effects. Ink applied to acetate and allowed to dry can be scratched out. This technique is a variation of "scratchboard." Scratchboard is waterproof ink applied over specially prepared illustration board (see page 45). The acetate version is favored by illustrators because it can be used with a lightbox.

Another ink experiment uses rubber cement as the drawing medium. Dripping and brushing rubber cement onto illustration board is fun but not very precise. This technique produces accidents, surprises, and textures. Apply rubber cement to a board and let it dry completely. Then, brush India ink over the whole area. The rubber cement will protect the paper from the ink. When the ink is dry, use a rubber cement pickup to lift the rubber cement off the paper.

Another version of this technique uses white watercolor paint instead of rubber cement (see page 44 for complete instruction). This is often called the "fake woodcut" or "washaway" technique, because the final effect resembles a woodcut.

Waterproof ink on illustration board

Technical illustration is a term for drawings that convey mechanical, architectural, and other scientific (or technical) information. These drawings may be very simple, such as instructions for assembling a paper kite. Or they may be complicated, such as a cutaway illustration of an engine that would appear in a manual on auto repair.

Take a close look at some of the technical pens (Rapidograph, Faber-Castell, Rotring, etc.) that can be used for technical work. They come with a variety of pen points, each of which produces an even and clean line. Many of these pens, because of their tiny, cylindrical points, must be held upright, especially when they are used with templates, curves, and other drafting aids.

Technical pen with templates and rulers on vellum tracing paper

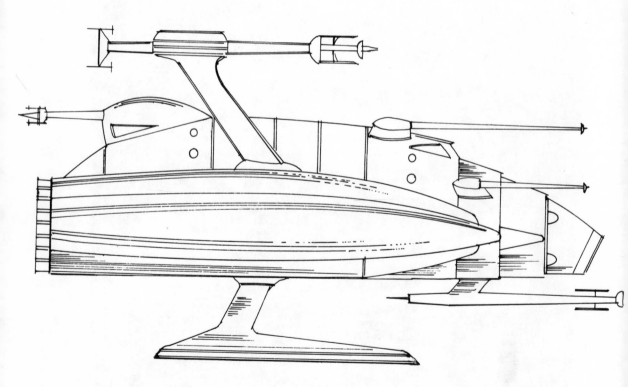

The drawings on these pages were done with a very fine (Triple-O Faber-Castell) pen. In these experiments, all the lines are clearly visible and separate. However, the same pen point was used to create the very fine textures on the armored figure in Chapter 4 (page 47). It was also the tool for achieving the cross-hatch effects on pages 52 and 58.

Illustrators, when they are familiar with all the pen-and-ink techniques, can use them in any way that is best suited to a particular job.

Technical pen with circle and oval templates and triangles on vellum tracing paper

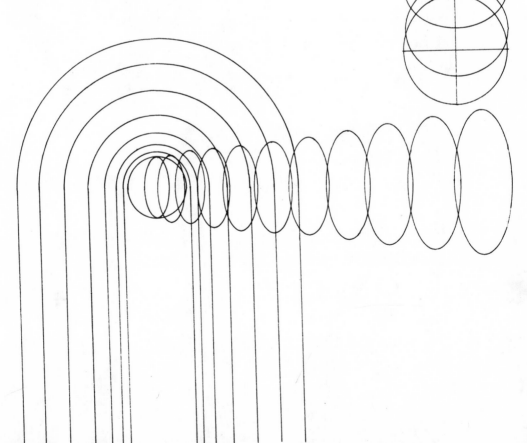

CHAPTER 3

The World Around Us

Have you noticed how curious people become when they see someone sketching? It doesn't matter whether the scene being sketched is a famous tourist attraction such as the Grand Canyon or just the passengers on the other side of the bus. We are all eager to know what has caught the artist's eye. Usually when we see the sketch, we are surprised because the artist has singled out or emphasized something that has escaped our attention.

This brief and wordless exchange between the artist and an onlooker illustrates one of the most satisfying things about art—the sharing of a vision. Through the sketch, the artist quietly but clearly expresses a point of view about the world around us.

When the sketching tool is a pen, the opportunity for expressive drawing is greater because the artist cannot erase "mistakes." These so-called mistakes are a recording of the artist's search for what is most meaningful. One of the wonders of art is that each of a dozen artists sketching the same scene will draw it differently. Another surprise is that if you draw the same scene twelve times, it will never be the same. If you want to experiment even further, try using a different type of pen each time you draw the same scene. You may discover ways of looking and sketching that had never occurred to you.

Fountain pen (fine point) on newsprint

Above: *very fine felt-tipped pen on sketchbook paper;* right: *felt brush pen on bond*

The nice thing about drawing in the park is that you have plenty of models: people on benches, children on swings, joggers, ball players. Wherever you look there are many different activities.

Bring a sketchbook or pad, a fountain pen, and/or a felt pen and begin by trying to capture basic positions and action. Remember you are *not* going to worry about "mistakes." Draw what you see. Work quickly—don't even lift the pen off the paper. It's the attitude of the figure that you want, not its details. Drawing from life, as this is called, develops your ability to concentrate on what is important in a scene.

An illustrator must select only those elements that will most clearly convey the meaning and mood of the story. Often, it is a small gesture or stance that best tells the story.

Drawings from a sketchbook. These were done with fiber-tipped pens on bond.

The world around us is full of fascinating objects. And it seems that many of them are on exhibit at flea markets. From an illustrator's point of view, a flea market is a treasure trove. There, along with odd clocks, broken crockery, and old clothes, an illustrator can also find wonderful models. The people at a flea market, both buyers and sellers, are so absorbed in what they are doing that they are completely unaware of your sketching.

Draw, just as you did at the park, quickly, rarely lifting the pen off the paper. If it is the objects that attract you, draw only those details that appeal to you. You should fill your notebooks with as many impressions as you can. Take along several types of pens, perhaps with different size points. Fountain pens have to be refilled so remember to take extra ink. Carry all of this in a small toolbox and, if you can, bring a small folding chair or stool. Date all your sketches and make notes. In this way, these sketchbooks will become your own reference library.

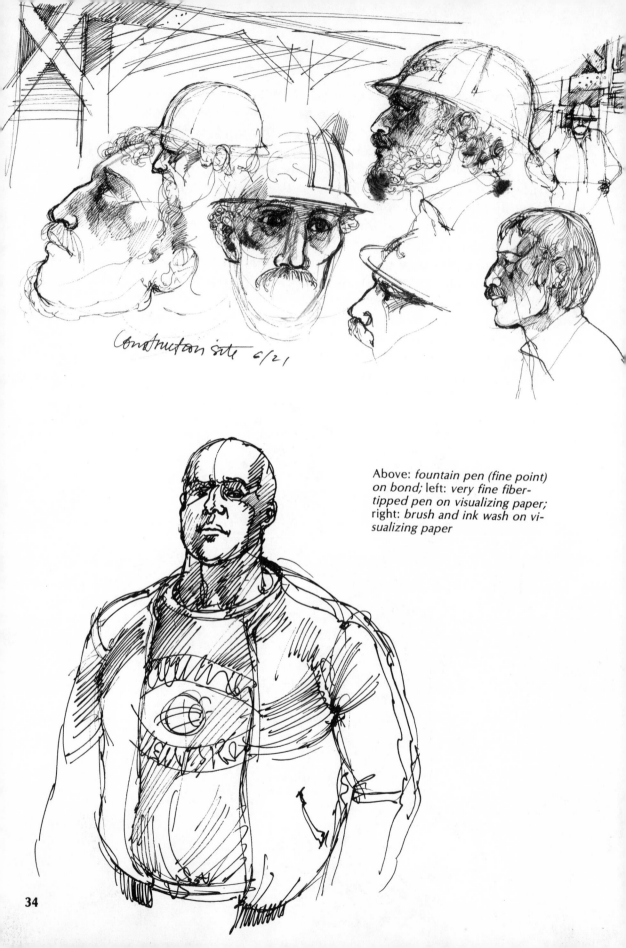

Construction site 6/21

Above: *fountain pen (fine point) on bond;* left: *very fine fiber-tipped pen on visualizing paper;* right: *brush and ink wash on visualizing paper*

Most illustrators enjoy studying the faces of people around them. Whenever possible they will sketch interesting characters they encounter. Sometimes an illustrator will visit a particular place to get faces for a specific project. These preliminary drawings for a story on labor unions in a large city were drawn at a construction site. Often a character will simply stand out as someone who should be recorded in a sketchbook. The weight lifter was observed in a subway car.

If no sketchbook is handy, an illustrator will make mental notes of a face and put it on paper as soon as possible. That is how the ink-wash drawing of the young woman was done. She was observed in a hospital waiting room.

The important point of these drawings is that each of the faces seems to have a story. Trying to capture the facial characteristics and expressions that will tell that story is one of the most challenging aspects of illustration.

Annie from life

a. 2H-2B pencil on bond paper; b. fine fiber-tipped pen with gray broad-tipped felt markers; c. fountain pen (fine point) on visualizing paper; d. fiber-tipped pen on visualizing paper

a.

Up to now we've been discussing the importance of the quick sketch. You've seen how pen sketches can help you develop your coordination. Sharpening your eye for details and gestures will help you capture on paper all sorts of characters.

There is another approach to drawing, one with different requirements. This type of drawing is more studied. It takes more time, includes the use of pencil, and requires more cooperation between artist and model.

The ink drawings on these pages were all done from an original pencil study of the model (see illustration reduced from original size). That drawing took several hours and was intended as a basic, three-dimensional study of the head. The artist was concerned with the basic structure because he knew the pencil study would have to serve as a model for future drawings. This is one way that illustrators prepare. A file of such drawings is one of the best reference sources for an illustrator. With this drawing as a guide, the artist merely has to trace (on a lightbox) a few key lines in pencil onto the papers intended for the ink drawings.

After that, the illustrator is free to experiment with different pen-and-ink effects without the worry of ruining the original.

c.

d.

Left and below: *technical pen
(fine point) on bond.* Right: *fountain pen (fine point) with ink wash
and white paint for highlights on
bond paper*

When you feel more confident working with this medium, you should attempt a portrait directly in pen and ink without a preliminary pencil drawing. Begin with a profile. Warn your model that the drawing will take a while. Use a pen with a fine point. You'll need this to create tones and shading.

Don't worry about getting a likeness of your model. What is most important to an illustrator is that the drawing has a strong sense of structure and form. Sometimes it is a good idea to leave some areas open (white). These provide a contrast to the textures created by the fine pen strokes.

Try adding a light wash of ink to one of your drawings. This is another way to create a sense of structure. The final effect should convince you and your audience that you've drawn a real person.

C H A P T E R 4

Expanding Your Imagination

Would you like to capture your dreams on paper? A famous artist claimed that he always went to bed with a pen and pad by his side, while holding a dish in his outstretched hand. As he fell asleep the dish would slip from his hand, crash onto the floor, and awaken him. In this way, he hoped to sketch his dreams quickly just as they were happening!

Artists are always trying to remember and record that elusive kind of imagery. Our imaginations work so quickly that it is difficult to retain specific visions. They are usually gone before we can get pen and paper in hand. Nevertheless, we keep trying.

We doodle. It is fun and relaxing. Everyone does doodles, but for artists they offer clues to even bigger pictures tucked away in the farthest corners of their imaginations.

We can look at what other artists are doing: in books, galleries, museums. We can take our own work and lay it all out before us, comparing one drawing with another. We can try combining elements from several drawings into one, and we may even surprise ourselves with the strange results.

All sketches done with fountain pen or fiber-tipped pen on bond

Sometimes a doodle just grows and grows—until it becomes a story. Freddy Cat began life as a doodle on the margin of a sketchbook. Then Freddy visited a party—before the other guests had arrived. The pen that drew Freddy finally got him home and into bed, but it was too late! Freddy had eaten too many goodies. . . . "Feed him to the sharks," yelled the pirates. But the doodling pen ran out of space; there was nothing to do but wake up Freddy.

Doodling can be done with any pen, but it's easier with pens that don't need frequent refilling.

Fiber-tipped pen on visualizing paper

Since you've just come from Freddy's nightmare, maybe you would like to try creating one of your own. Two techniques mentioned earlier (Chapter 2) are ideal for "Monster Making." First try the fake woodcut (or washaway) technique. Do two drawings: a human face and an animal face (pick an animal that scares you). You can do two separate washaways (like the example) and then combine them in a third picture. Or, you can combine the two heads on tracing paper and use the washaway technique for the final picture.

Here are the steps:

1. Do a light pencil drawing of the design on two-ply paper.

2. Paint (white or gray watercolor) around the edge of the lines of the pictures. Everything *not* painted will end up black, and painted areas will remain white.

3. Let the paint dry completely.

4. Brush India ink (waterproof) quickly over the entire area (painted and non-painted). Do not brush back and forth over paint.

5. When dry, run water over the paper; the paint will wash away.

6. Do not create these monsters before going to bed or when there is a full moon.

Scratchboard is ideal for monster fantasies because the scene can be set at night and all the creatures will seem to glow. One caution: Don't dig too deeply into the surface of the paper or it will tear.

This page: *waterproof ink on two-ply Strathmore kid finish.* Opposite: *prepared scratchboard*

44

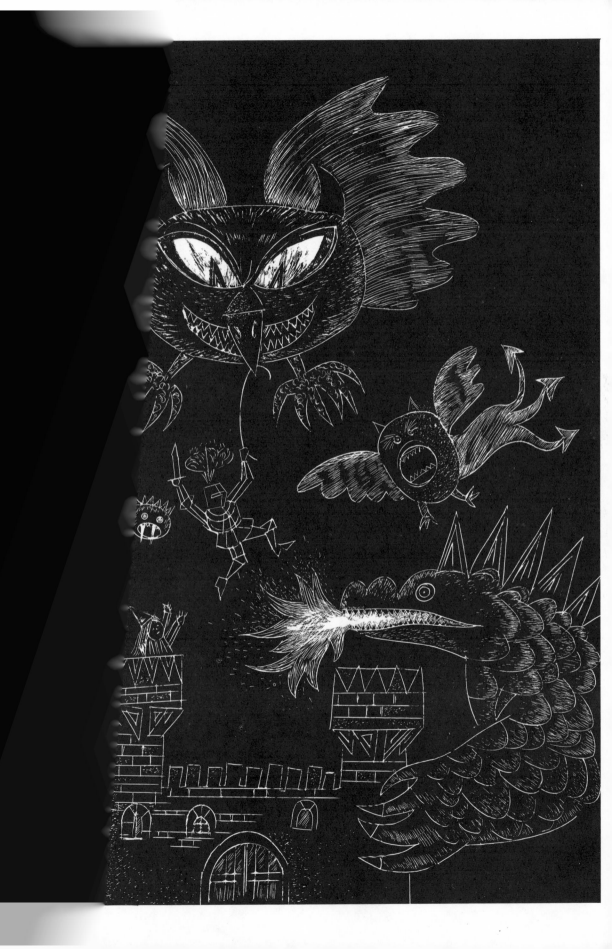

Fairy tales, myths, fantasy, and science fiction are subjects that take us beyond our everyday existence. They allow us to imagine worlds filled with enchanted creatures and magical powers.

The drawing on this page is right out of a sketchbook. It was done simply because it interested the artist. When the illustrator received the assignment to draw the enchanted knight this sketch and others (of horses and armor) were her references.

The artist treated the subject matter seriously. Unlike Freddy's adventure or the other drawings in this chapter, this illustration is intended to be serious rather than funny. Do you think that the technique and the artist's handling of dark and light add to the drama? Asking questions about other illustrators' work will help you make decisions about your own work.

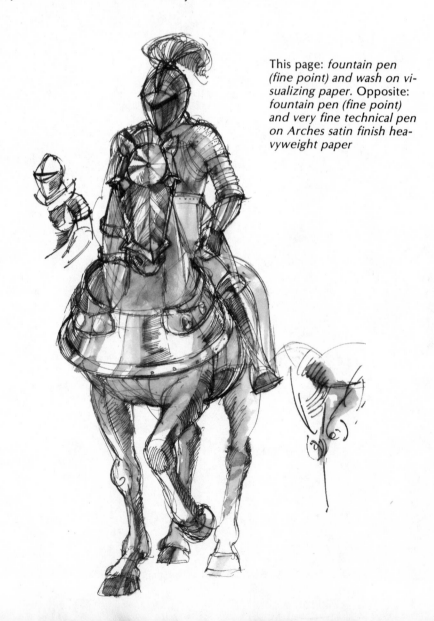

This page: *fountain pen (fine point) and wash on visualizing paper.* Opposite: *fountain pen (fine point) and very fine technical pen on Arches satin finish heavyweight paper*

Another exercise for your imagination is drawing things that are either absurd or totally out of scale. The drawings on these pages and on pages 50–51 are examples of both. A lion and a mouse really don't belong in the same picture. But if they are there, what do you do with them? Having a lion run from a mouse is absurd—but fables and children's stories are filled with similar situations.

Doing this kind of drawing exercise with an unusual pen will be another experience. This frantic lion was drawn with a felt brush, a tool that is full of surprises.

Felt brush marker on newsprint

Fountain pen (fine point) and crowquill on visualizing paper

Now for a pleasant evening of chamber music. Maestro Mouse taps his baton, Miss Hippo, the first violinist, tunes up the orchestra, and we sit back ready to enjoy the music and the costumes.

The illustrator enjoys drawing historical costumes and animals that do what people do. So, why not combine the two and dress the animals in historical costumes?

But why an orchestra? No special reason, other than the artist's love of music. It could have been a parade, a circus, a disco, a banquet, a ballgame, anything—whatever subject you enjoy drawing.

These drawings are just the beginning. When an artist's imagination starts working, no one, not even the artist, can predict what will happen.

C H A P T E R 5

Sketch to Finish

When does a drawing become an illustration? One answer is when that drawing tells a specific story in a distinct way. Both its story and its style contribute to the mood or feeling of an illustration.

We've demonstrated some of the steps an artist takes toward achieving a style. You've seen experiments with various materials and techniques that develop a personal approach to pen and ink. You know, now, that drawing skills are as necessary as good technique and that expanding your imagination is as important as producing a convincing figure drawing.

The practice of these skills will make you a better artist. But, to become an illustrator, to turn a drawing into an illustration, requires something else. Remember Chapter 4? Recall how ideas and notes and doodles were combined to produce unusual and unpredictable results. The different elements were chosen to produce specific pictures, which meant that the artist had to decide what to put in or leave out of each illustration. This part of picture making is referred to by many words such as selection, organization, composition, design. The exact word is not important. What is important is learning how to make this design process work for you.

Fountain pen (medium point) and technical pen (fine point) with gray marker on bond paper

Fountain pen (fine point) and fiber-tipped pen on bond paper

Every illustrator has his or her own method for making decisions, but most illustrators start the same way.

After getting an assignment, an illustrator begins sketching. Many of these first sketches are small and rough and are meant to be seen only by the illustrator. These "thumbnails" (as such sketches are called) are visual notes that explore various ways of doing the job. For example, the sketches on pages 54 through 57 represent different approaches to the assignment (creating an illustration with "mystery"). The story had an old house and barn, a full moon, the sea, and a main character who was a young girl. The illustrator had to use one or more of these story elements in the picture.

After reading the story, the illustrator started doing thumbnails. He did more than one because it is rare that the first idea is the one that is finally used. From these early thumbnails, we've selected several to demonstrate how the process works.

One way to get started is to move the elements around. Sometimes include the whole figure. Try using only the face in the foreground. Or, leave the girl out entirely and focus on the house or part of the house. At times during this exploration phase, one idea will have special appeal. Then the artist may do a larger sketch, even working out a detail or two (right).

Another method is to sketch with a medium unlike the one intended for use on the finished illustration. Sometimes this will introduce a totally new approach; the pencil sketch (above) suggested the possibility of doing the illustration as a wash drawing.

In any case, the greatest benefit of sketches, thumbnail and otherwise, is that you, the artist, are given an opportunity to be critical of your own ideas. You must be able to say to yourself, "Well, I thought that was a good idea, but now that I see it, it's not what I want."

The illustrator of these pictures did just that. After evaluating his sketches, he chose the large window to work up as a possible finished illustration. The artist also did some research in his picture library. This file can contain almost anything that could be basic research material for illustration: magazine clippings, books, photos, and, of course, the artist's own sketchbooks.

In one of these he found a pen-and-wash drawing of an old barn; there was even a moon reflected in the window (page 56). This old sketch became the basis for the second version (page 58) of the "mystery" illustration. Now the illustrator had two finished "mystery" pictures.

Opposite page, top: *fountain pen (fine point) and fiber-tipped pen on bond paper.* Opposite page, bottom: *crowquill, wash and white paint on watercolor paper.* Bottom: *fiber-tipped pen on visualizing paper*

Which one do you think the illustrator chose? Which one would you have picked, or would you have chosen one of the other ideas?

Below: *crowquill, technical pen, and wash on visualizing paper.* Opposite page: *fountain pen (fine point) and crowquill on visualizing paper*

Above: *fiber-tipped pen on visualizing paper.* Opposite page: *fountain pen (medium point), dip pen (fine point), and wash on visualizing paper*

As you can see, deciding between one drawing and another is not easy. But these are decisions that illustrators must make all the time. How does an illustrator choose between two equally interesting drawings?

An illustrator must go back to the original sketches. The sequence of illustrations on pages 60–63 is a good example. For this assignment the artist was asked to do a drawing of one of the main characters from *Treasure Island*. His first sketches were simple thumbnails that showed the various ways of composing the picture. But the sketches were too small to help him determine which pen and ink technique to use. For that purpose, the artist did several full-size sketches. One of them (page 61), a combination of pen and wash that created a mysterious and sinister atmosphere, appealed to him.

However, after looking at it and thinking about it for several days, the artist decided that the pirate's face needed more character and texture. To achieve this, the artist eliminated the wash and used only line. He also experimented with leaving out the second pirate and the boat. It was clear that these elements were competing with the main character.

The result is a picture, created with a variety of lines and cross-hatch, of two flinty characters who glare straight at the reader with eyes that are mean, and not to be trusted.

What began as an idea, then a sketch, finally becomes an illustration; a picture that tells a story—with style.

The world of illustration is large and boundless. It begins with the treasures of literature and extends to the limits of your imagination. To explore this world, you need nothing more than a few simple tools—and desire.

Fountain pen (fine point), crowquill, and technical pen on Fabriano smooth finish paper

Index

Bristol board, 13

Calligraphy, 9, 10
Cartridge pen, 10
Comp preparation, 15
Cross-hatching, 19, 20, 27

Design process, 54
Dip pens, 10, 17
Doodles, 41, 43
Drafting tools, 17
Drawing from life, 30

Effects, experimenting for, 19–28

Faces, drawing, 35
Fake woodcut technique, 25, 44
Felt pens, 14
Fountain pens, 10
French curve, 17

Goose quills, 9

Illustration, 7, 53
Imagination, expanding, 41–52
Ink wash, 34
Inks, 9, 10, 13, 24

Lampblack, 9
Ledger board, 13
Lightbox, 17, 21

Materials, 9–18
Monster making, 44

Nibs, 9, 10

Out of scale drawings, 48

Paper, 13, 17
Pencil studies, 36
Penholders, 10
Pens, 9–10, 22
Personal approach, 53
Point of view, artist's, 29
Portraits, 34

Reference sources, 36
Reservoir pen, 10
Rubber cement, as drawing medium, 13, 24–25
Ruling pens, 17

Scratchboard, 24, 44
Sketch to finish, 53–63
Sketchboards, 30, 33
Studied drawing, 36
Style, developing, 53

T square, 17
Technical illustration, 17, 26
Technical paper, 17, 26–27
Techniques, 21
Templates, 17
Thumbnail sketches, 54
Tones, creating with inks, 13
Triangles, 17

Vellum tracing paper, 13

Washaway technique, 25, 44
White watercolor paint, as drawing medium, 25
World around us, 29–40